A Biblical Response to Cults

CONCORDIA PUBLISHING HOUSE · SAINT LOUIS

3558 S. Jefferson Ave., St. Louis, MO 63118-3968
1-800-325-3040 • cph.org

Written by Jesse Yow

Manufactured in the United States of America

1 2 3 4 5 6 7 8 9 10 31 30 29 28 27 26 25 24 23 22

WHAT IS A CULT?

Sometimes we see a friend, relative, or neighbor involved in what looks like a sincere religion, but while it claims to be Christian, something seems off. Not just unfamiliar, but somehow different in terms of content or focus. How do we know if it is a faithful form of Christianity or a cult? To find out whether a religious movement is a cult or is authentically Christian, let's turn to the Sunday School answer: Jesus.

In John 14:6, Jesus said, "I am the way, and the truth, and the life. No one comes to the Father except through Me." This clear, pithy statement gives us a simple litmus test: if a religious movement claims to be Christian but teaches some way of salvation or way to God other than Jesus, then it is a cult. If it draws people away from the truth that is Jesus, the living Word of God, then it is a cult. If it substitutes life under the group's leader or life in the movement for life in Jesus, then it is a cult. In summary, cults are "organizations or movements that represent deviant expressions of the central and foundational teachings of Christianity."[1] Jesus, and nothing else, is the center of authentic Christianity.

WHAT'S THE PROBLEM?

We need to take cults seriously because they involve matters of spiritual life and death—and sometimes physical life and death. Cults can harm their participants and, in a ripple effect, the families and friends of their participants. Cults are often also deceptive, such that participants may not realize the danger until it is too late. Perhaps the best way to see the problem is through a few examples or case histories.

A dynamic leader, Jim Jones established the Peoples Temple[2] in San Francisco in 1956. Jones

---

1 "Cults—An Overview," LCMS Commission on Theology and Church Relations, April 2005, p. 1, https://files.lcms.org/wl/?id=YgWwnCV9lL3JR3ty0tYNmgmiUQKYa4IU.

2 "Commentary: 35 Years after Jonestown," *The LCMS Reporter*, November 15, 2013.

preached an attractive mix of economic justice and spiritual fulfillment and gradually built a large following of people seeking salvation, eternal life, and utopia. His movement grew, and Jones moved the group to Guyana in 1973 to reduce the opportunity for public scrutiny and to avoid US laws. Once in Guyana, he named their isolated compound Jonestown in honor of himself. Jones manipulated his followers through brainwashing and forced labor, leading the families of members of the Peoples Temple to become more and more alarmed about the fate of their loved ones. As concerns grew, a member of the US Congress led a visit to the Peoples Temple in 1978 to see the situation firsthand. At the end of the visit, Jones ordered the murder of the congressman and the staff and news reporters who had accompanied him. Once the murders were complete, Jones then ordered the murder and forced suicide of every Peoples Temple member in Jonestown, leading to the deaths of 918 men, women, and children.

Our second example involves a cult known as Heaven's Gate. This relatively small cult combined a deviation from Scripture based on the Jesus Seminar[3] with an old heresy known as Gnosticism. The first part led cult participants to put their own authority above that of God's Word; the second part rationalized that our bodies are only temporary, corrupt "containers" for our souls. The Jesus Seminar part of the Heaven's Gate belief system denied the reality and significance of Jesus' atoning death and bodily resurrection; the Gnostic part advocated that physical death is the beneficial gateway to spiritual perfection and heaven. Synthesized and taken to the extreme in the Heaven's Gate cult, this belief system led to the group suicide of thirty-nine adults in Rancho Santa Fe, California.[4]

For a third example, we turn to another small, recent cult known as The Body or the Attleboro

---

3 Starting in the 1980s, the Jesus Seminar was a group of people, primarily academics, who denied the inerrancy and inspiration of the Bible. They met to debate how much of Jesus' words and actions in the Gospels were authentic, eventually declaring that over 80 percent of Jesus' recorded deeds and speech were inauthentic.

4 "Hell at Heaven's Gate," *World Magazine*, April 12, 1997, https://wng.org/articles/hell-at-heavens-gate-1617646282.

cult. With up to forty members in Attleboro, Massachusetts, this cult came into being when a few families left their local church and Bible studies to start their own home church. They believed that they had received special revelations and scriptural understanding from God that set them apart from the historic, orthodox Christian Church. In fact, they saw themselves as the only true Christians left on earth. Their isolated world came apart, though, when a cult member's prophecy led them to starve a ten-month-old child to death. Police investigations led to a murder conviction and prison sentences.[5]

A fourth, even more modern example involves a cult that revolves around a Messiah-like leader, even though it does not explicitly embrace any particularly Christian beliefs. NXIVM started as a professional development group but evolved quickly into a self-improvement cult involving racketeering, sex trafficking, slave labor, and other

---

5 Candi Cushman, "Fatal Revelation: How a Small 'Christian' Bible Study Group Turned into a Deadly Cult," *World Magazine*, February 17, 2001, https://wng.org/articles/fatal-revelation-1617340233, and Emily Belz, "When the Fog Lifts," *World Magazine*, June 29, 2019, https://wng.org/articles/when-the-fog-lifts-1620590821.

crimes. Its founder, Keith Raniere, ruled the cult through a hierarchy of associates. As a purported self-help group, it taught a false form of salvation based on total submission to the leader of the cult.[6]

As we look for common threads in these four examples, we see that cults are dangerous for their participants. Sadly, while details may differ from one cult to another, outcomes for participants often involve physical or emotional abuse, manipulation, sexual abuse (incest, pedophilia, rape, or sexual assault), enslavement, mass suicide, or murder. By diverting their members from salvation found only in Jesus, cults lead people away from God's promise of eternal life. If your family members, friends, or neighbors become involved with a cult, they are at risk even though they may not realize it. And if you bring up the risks, they will probably become defensive or even angry as they deny it.

6 Deanna Paul, "Nxivm Founder Keith Raniere Sentenced to 120 Years," *The Wall Street Journal*, October 27, 2020, and Mimi Nguyen Ly, "Keith Raniere, NXIVM Cult Leader, Ordered to Pay $3.5 Million to Victims," *The Epoch Times*, July 21, 2021.

Cults pose another danger early in a person's involvement by attracting and entrapping him or her. Nobody wakes up in the morning and says, "What a beautiful morning! I think I will join a cult today!" Instead, the cult draws people in as they seek spiritual truth, fulfillment, self-improvement, comfort, friendship, or emotional support. As their entanglement with the cult grows, they are deceived, isolated, and manipulated. If these people are not well-grounded in Scripture, it is easy for them to be deceived by false teaching, a charismatic leader, or both.

WHAT ARE CULTS LIKE?

Cults come and go, historically speaking, and they appear in different shapes and sizes. However, cults have many spiritual, sociological, and psychological characteristics in common:

- *Charismatic, authoritarian leaders.* A cult leader may display an attractive, dynamic personality to entice followers and assert authority. This personality may be real or a facade. For example, the Peoples Temple, described briefly above, grew around the captivating personality of Jim Jones. Alternatively, cult leaders may attract followers with claims of a new revelation of truth, since potential followers may find their teaching (see next item) more attractive than their personality. Their leadership usually avoids accountability to peers or superiors. In fact, they probably believe that they have no peers or superiors. Implicitly or explicitly, they may not acknowledge any accountability to God, although they may give the matter nominal lip service. While genuine Christian leaders are quick to give God thanks and glory, cult leaders may not even mention Jesus, much less acknowledge His lordship.

- *Claims of a new revelation of truth.* Cults invariably teach a distorted view of biblical truth, a version that leaves out key parts of the truth, or a version that adds their own warped ideas to God's Word. Sometimes they assert special knowledge by claiming to have prophecies, revelations, or new truths that add to the Bible or that go beyond what the Bible teaches. For example, The Body, mentioned above, set aside much of the Bible in favor of living by special revelations in the form of prophecy from a few assertive cult members. Larger cults may even publish their own version of scriptures and teach that the Bible used by orthodox Christians is corrupt and unreliable. Typically, cult teaching involves some form of salvation by works, and of course, the works necessary for salvation (however they define salvation) require joining and supporting the cult. In essence, they replace salvation in Christ with some other form of salvation defined on their terms rather than by God.

- *Demand for total allegiance.* Loyalty to the cult, its teachings, and its leadership are paramount. Any deviation from complete loyalty meets with disapproval, discipline, or punishment. A cult's demands for allegiance preclude questions, doubts, and any ideas that do not conform to cult doctrines. Just as the rigors of boot camp force an inductee to submit to military training, cults may impose extreme rules for daily living to suppress personal identity, sap the will to resist, and force the new member into submission. Sometimes the discipline affects members who are helpless to resist, such as the young child who starved to death in The Body as part of the discipline imposed by the cult.

- *Sowing distrust and even hatred of the outside world.* As part of their campaign to immerse members in their way of thought and prevent them from leaving, cults will often teach members to distrust nonmembers, including family and friends. They may teach members to "make nice" and pretend everything is okay when talking with nonmembers, even while teaching members that they cannot trust nonmembers. They may teach that anyone outside the cult will be dishonest and untrustworthy because they believe false teaching (and any teaching other than what the cult believes is, by definition, false teaching). In extreme cases, the cult may teach members to hate or fear nonmembers, possibly leading to a sense of paranoia about any person, group, or organization outside of the cult. In the Peoples Temple example, this hatred and paranoia led to mass suicide.

- *Isolation from outside influence.* As part of their methods for keeping members in their grip, cult leaders usually impose some degree of isolation from outside influence. This might include cutting off relationships with friends and relatives, stopping access to the internet (including social media, news, and even email), blocking the news and other broadcast media, and especially blocking uncontrolled interactions with people outside the cult. In extreme cases, the cult may physically move some or all of its members to remote locations or walled enclosures. To name two examples, the Peoples Temple moved from the US to Guyana to block the influence of friends, family, counselors, and law enforcement personnel, and the Branch Davidians moved into a fortified compound in Texas to avoid external influences.

- *Emphasis on fundraising and recruitment.* Cults usually self-organize into a caste system in which newer and lower-level members support the cult leadership both financially and with their work. Scientology, for example, charges members fees for training as they become more involved in the cult and as they move up through the ranks.[7] Cults also put members to work in fundraising or in proselytizing people to join the cult. These tasks often count as part of the salvation by works practiced by the cult. They may use door-to-door visitation in what amounts to sales calls as part of their recruiting. Alternatively, they may seek donations and new recruits at book tables or information booths in public places such as airport lobbies, bus stops, and libraries. Typically, a more senior cult member will

7 Mark Bergin, "Superpower Religion," *World Magazine*, May 27, 2006, https://wng.org/articles/superpower-religion-1617617803.

work with new members, both as part of the member's training and to keep the members from straying from cult teachings if they happen to meet an articulate Christian.

- *Manipulating emotions to prevent critical or independent thought.* As a member falls under the influence of the cult, the cult leaders, teachers, and mentors will use peer pressure; feelings of sympathy, guilt, or pride; and factors such as fatigue or hunger to manipulate and control the person. This approach aims to draw the member further into the cult's teachings; prevent critical questioning, second-guessing, or unguided thinking; and increase susceptibility and acceptance for the cult's teachings and practices. This eventually crushes or at least sets aside the member's will and independence. For example, senior members of The Body pressured the rest of the cult to accept prophecies by one or two cult leaders as newly revealed truth. This led to the death of a child by starvation and criminal prosecution of cult leadership once the event came to light.

- *Creating feelings of fear and dependency.* Along with emotional manipulation, cults may try to make members fearful of outsiders, particularly those who do not buy in to cult beliefs and who may be able to make the case for orthodox Christianity. As part of their discipline and manipulation, cults will try to keep their members emotionally dependent on the cult and its sense of community, and they may try to keep their members physically dependent on the cult. Emotional dependency includes personal security, sense of worth, acceptance, and fulfillment. The cult will teach members that they will begin to lose these things if they question or doubt the cult and its leadership, and they will suffer worse if they step away from commitment to the cult. Physical dependency might include relying on the cult for food, clothing, and housing, and the same principles of control apply: toe the line with the cult, or you lose your support. Heaven's Gate and the other cults cited above each employed these techniques of emotional dependency and manipulation as part of their assimilation of new members.

- *Redefining common religious terms.* As cults deviate from roots found in orthodox Christianity, they will often continue to use religious words and concepts but with new meanings, distorted to fit their own teachings. The best way to bring this distortion to light is through questions. For example, if the cult uses words such as *faith* or *belief*, what is the source of the faith or the specific object of belief? The Bible says that faith is a gift of God, and simply put, Jesus is the object of Christian belief. A cult, on the other hand, may mean belief in self (like the self-improvement of Scientology) or faith in a cult's founder (a person, but not Jesus). Similarly, the cult may speak of spiritual growth or improvement, but does this mean Christian discipleship and sanctification, or does it mean following a charismatic cult leader into self-improvement? The cult may go to great lengths to hide its differences from biblical Christianity with semantics and word games, so it may take some probing and careful defining of terms to bring those differences to light.

We often give people and ministries the benefit of the doubt, particularly if they claim to be Christian. How do we recognize when a group is leading people away from Jesus Christ and into slavery to false teaching? On what basis can we challenge the false teaching, call it what it is, and attempt to help friends, family members, or neighbors see the truth?

SCRIPTURE AS OUR RULE AND GUIDE

If you ask a banker how to spot counterfeit money, he or she will reply that you first need to know how to recognize genuine money. You must know what real money looks like. Similarly, we first need to know what God's Word teaches before we can recognize when a cult or its leaders deviate from God's truth.

Deviations found in cults usually involve adding to God's Word, subtracting from God's Word, or in some way denying revealed truth about God. Adding to God's Word might involve claims of new insights that twist or distort the meaning of Scripture. For example, the cult might readily endorse the idea of salvation by God's grace, as found in Ephesians 2:8–10,[8] but it might then twist verse 10 to add that performing works assigned by the cult is necessary to win its distorted view of salvation. We do not use loose-leaf Bibles that allow us to add new revelations according to every whim of heresy, but a cult might claim new revelations that carry more weight than the canonical Scriptures. In the cult's rationale, those new revelations clarify obscure passages or correct supposed corruptions of Scripture.

---

8 Ephesians 2:8–10 says, "For by grace you have been saved through faith. And this is not your own doing; it is the gift of God, not a result of works, so that no one may boast. For we are His workmanship, created in Christ Jesus for good works, which God prepared beforehand, that we should walk in them."

Some cults will effectively subtract from God's Word by, for example, denying that Jesus is fully God or that He is fully man. In defiance of John 1:1, 14[9] or 1 John 4:1–3,[10] the cult may teach that Jesus was only a good man, and one that cult members should follow, but certainly not God in flesh. Or instead, the cult may teach that Jesus was a pure spiritual being, but certainly not human.

Some cults deviate from God's revealed truth by denying the Trinity. They may claim that the Father, Son, and Holy Spirit are mutually exclusive modes in which God chooses to act, as if God puts off one mode and puts on another like a quick-change artist. Since this makes it difficult to explain passages like Luke 3:21–22,[11] in which

---

9 John 1:1 says, "In the beginning was the Word, and the Word was with God, and the Word was God," and John 1:14 adds, "And the Word became flesh and dwelt among us, and we have seen His glory, glory as of the only Son from the Father, full of grace and truth."

10 The Bible says in 1 John 4:1–3, "Beloved, do not believe every spirit, but test the spirits to see whether they are from God, for many false prophets have gone out into the world. By this you know the Spirit of God: every spirit that confesses that Jesus Christ has come in the flesh is from God, and every spirit that does not confess Jesus is not from God. This is the spirit of the antichrist, which you heard was coming and now is in the world already."

11 Luke 3:21–22 says, "Now when all the people were baptized, and when Jesus also had been baptized and was praying, the heavens were opened, and the Holy Spirit descended on Him in bodily form, like a dove; and a voice came from heaven, 'You are My beloved Son; with You I am well pleased.'"

the Father, Son, and Holy Spirit each appear at the Baptism of Jesus, they will find some way to minimize or deny that passage. On the other hand, they may claim that the Father, Son, and Holy Spirit are three separate gods, in defiance of Deuteronomy 6:4[12] and its uses in the New Testament. In any of these situations, the cult leads its members away from God's revealed truth and into a theology of the cult's own making.

We need to use Scripture as our rule and guide to be able to spot a cult's deviant teaching and, when given the opportunity, counter or correct it. Acts 17:11 sets an example for us, saying, "Now these Jews were more noble than those in Thessalonica; they received the word with all eagerness, examining the Scriptures daily to see if these things were so."

In other words, they checked even the apostle Paul against God's Word, using Scripture as the gold standard for truth. For us to do this effectively, we need to know what the Bible teaches.

---

12 Deuteronomy 6:4 proclaims, "Hear, O Israel: The Lord our God, the Lord is one." This truth shows up in the New Testament in references such as Mark 12:29; John 17:3; and 1 Corinthians 8:4, 6.

Breaking this down, it means we need to know key Scripture passages and the doctrines they teach, and we need to know the rest of the Bible well enough to avoid falling victim to a cult's proof text of Bible verses used out of context. But if we do not already have this level of knowledge and understanding, where do we turn?

Fortunately, God gives us resources for help in knowing Scripture and in knowing the real thing when it comes to spiritual truth. First, of course, is our personal Bible, particularly a good study Bible such as *The Lutheran Study Bible*. Second, talk with your pastor. He speaks and teaches God's truth, and he also knows how to spot and counter spiritual heresies and deviations from God's Word. Third, go to *Luther's Small Catechism with Explanation* for a concise, well-organized presentation of important truths from Scripture. The Small Catechism comes with exhaustive Scripture references and explanations and provides a good start on refreshing your understanding of God's truth.

KEY TEACHINGS OF SCRIPTURE

At this point, let us step back to review a few key theological topics we should have in mind to be able to identify and resist a cult's false teaching. These include salvation by grace, not works; Jesus as true God and true man; God's plan for redemption; and the nature and role of the Church. Let's briefly reflect on each of these.

- *Salvation by grace, not works.* Romans 3 states that every human being is a sinner and needs salvation from his or her guilt before God.[13] However, we cannot save ourselves. Therefore, as explained in Ephesians 2:4–10, God saves us by His grace and not by anything we do.[14] In fact, until God takes action

---

13 Romans 3:10–12 describes the situation for all humanity: "As it is written: 'None is righteous, no, not one; no one understands; no one seeks for God. All have turned aside; together they have become worthless; no one does good, not even one.'"

14 Ephesians 2:4–10 explains, "But God, being rich in mercy, because of the great love with which He loved us, even when we were dead in our trespasses, made us alive together with Christ—by grace you have been saved—and raised us up with Him and seated us with Him in the heavenly places in Christ Jesus, so that in the coming ages He might show the immeasurable riches of His grace in kindness toward us in Christ Jesus. For by grace you have been saved through faith. And this is not your own doing; it is the gift of God, not a result of works, so that no one may boast. For we are His workmanship, created in Christ Jesus for good works, which God prepared beforehand, that we should walk in them."

to save us, we are dead in our sins and cannot do anything to help or save ourselves. And John 3:16 tells why God sent Jesus to save us: because He loves us.[15] See the explanation of the Second Article of the Apostles' Creed in Luther's Small Catechism for more information.

- *Jesus as true God and true man.* Our Savior, Jesus, is God Incarnate. He is not half-God and half-man, or only a man, or only God; He is fully God and fully man. As noted above in references from John 1, Jesus is the Son of God who became flesh and dwelled among us. He suffered on the cross, died for our sins, and rose from the dead on the third day. Read through the first part of the explanation of the Second Article of the Apostles' Creed in Luther's Small Catechism for a more in-depth explanation.
- *God's plan for redemption.* John 3:16 explains God's plan for redemption in a nutshell, and

15 In John 3:16, Jesus explains, "For God so loved the world, that He gave His only Son, that whoever believes in Him should not perish but have eternal life."

Ephesians 2:4–10 amplifies that explanation. However, the roots of God's plan reach all the way back to Genesis 3:15, in which God promised to send someone who would crush the head of the one who tricked Adam and Eve into sin.[16] Jesus fulfilled this prophecy for us. God's plan also reaches forward to the end of time when, according to Revelation 21:1–4, He will establish the new heaven and the new earth.[17] As Romans 8:22–23 explains,[18] God has saved us in Christ, and yet we await the fulfillment of this salvation.

---

16 Although you should read Genesis 3:15 in the context of all of Genesis 3, the verse itself says, "I will put enmity between you and the woman, and between your offspring and her offspring; He shall bruise your head, and you shall bruise His heel."

17 Revelation 21:1–4 tells us what to expect at the end of time: "Then I saw a new heaven and a new earth, for the first heaven and the first earth had passed away, and the sea was no more. And I saw the holy city, new Jerusalem, coming down out of heaven from God, prepared as a bride adorned for her husband. And I heard a loud voice from the throne saying, 'Behold, the dwelling place of God is with man. He will dwell with them, and they will be His people, and God Himself will be with them as their God. He will wipe away every tear from their eyes, and death shall be no more, neither shall there be mourning, nor crying, nor pain anymore, for the former things have passed away.'"

18 Romans 8:22–23 states a paradox—we are already saved in Christ, yet we await the fulfillment of our salvation: "For we know that the whole creation has been groaning together in the pains of childbirth until now. And not only the creation, but we ourselves, who have the firstfruits of the Spirit, groan inwardly as we wait eagerly for adoption as sons, the redemption of our bodies."

- *Nature and role of the Church.* Acts 2:42 describes the Church as all believers, gathered in fellowship and prayer around God's teachings through the apostles.[19] Ephesians 4:4–6 emphasizes our unity in Christ and in fact describes us as the Body of Christ.[20] An individual Christian congregation or even a small group of believers is still part of the overall Body that is the Christian Church, the Body of Christ. Read through the second part of the explanation of the Third Article of the Apostles' Creed in Luther's Small Catechism for more information.

We may encounter other differences when we look into a cult's beliefs. Some will be trivial, while others may be quite significant. However, these key teachings from Scripture are likely to turn up as points of disagreement, and they serve as flags to proceed with caution. Now that we have brushed up on our understanding from God's Word, we are

19 Acts 2:42 says, "And they devoted themselves to the apostles' teaching and the fellowship, to the breaking of bread and the prayers."

20 Ephesians 4:4–6 says, "There is one body and one Spirit—just as you were called to the one hope that belongs to your call—one Lord, one faith, one baptism, one God and Father of all, who is over all and through all and in all."

in a better position to discern a cult's false teaching and respond with God's truth spoken in a spirit of love.

HOW CAN I HELP?

Our preparations for meeting a cult member, teacher, or leader must include time spent in prayer. Pray for understanding, discernment, protection, presence of mind, and clarity of thought and communication. Pray that the Holy Spirit will open the person's heart and mind to God's truth, that God's love for the lost will motivate what we say and how we listen, and that the Holy Spirit will guide our conversation. If we know about the discussion in advance, we should ask our pastor or one or two mature Christian friends to pray for us and for the conversation.

But what do we do when the person from the cult claims to understand Scripture better than we do, challenges us with questions we cannot readily answer, or simply proves to be obstinate? If our discussion with a cult member, teacher, or leader reaches a stalemate or becomes contentious, we may need to ask for time before responding to his or her challenges. We may need time to go back to the Bible, consult our pastor or another resource, or seek support from mature, committed Christian friends. Regardless, realize that this process will go according to God's timing rather than ours.

If family members, friends, or others you know begin talking about new teachings or exhibiting behaviors consistent with cult membership, you should try to investigate. First, do your homework. Ask questions to learn where they got those thoughts. Try to gently probe their meaning, both to show your concern and to discern the nature of any false teaching behind their words or behavior. In expressing interest, though, be careful not to create the impression that you agree with the false teaching or that you want to join them in the cult. As you scope out the situation, you will get a better idea of how to pray for them, what to ask or say, and what resources you need to consult to be able to help them.

Helping someone caught up in a cult will differ according to the circumstances, the person, and the nature of that particular cult. Therefore, as you begin to grasp the situation, seek advice from your pastor or perhaps an elder in your church on how best to help your friend. Your friend may also need physical assistance or guidance if he or she chooses to leave the cult.[21] However, while (or before) you get into the specifics of helping your friend, you will need to grapple with the false teaching in keeping with the discussion above. And you need to prepare to provide God's truth to take the place of the false teaching that, by God's grace, he or she will leave behind.

---

21 For more on this topic, see Jeffrey Mallinson, "How to Leave a Cult," July 2, 2019, https://www.protectyournoggin.org/articles/how-to-leave-a-cult.

WHERE CAN I LEARN MORE?

The Biblical Response series from Concordia Publishing House offers brief and easy-to-read summaries of important cultural topics for people who want to know what God's Holy Word says about cultural issues that touch our lives.

You can find additional information about cults in these resources:

- The Lutheran Church—Missouri Synod's Commission on Theology and Church Relations (CTCR) has published numerous short papers on various cults and religious groups online at https://www.lcms.org/about/leadership/commission-on-theology-and-church-relations/documents/religious-organizations-and-movements.
- The CTCR has also published an overview introduction to cults at https://files.lcms.org/wl/?id=YgWwnCV9lL3JR3tyotYNmgmiUQKYa4lU.

- The Faith on the Edge Bible study series published by Concordia Publishing House (CPH) provides useful information about cults, cultic behaviors, and similar kinds of deviant religious belief systems. *Faith and Science in a Skeptical Age*, also published by CPH, presents an update on this information in book rather than Bible study format.